SCRIPT WRITING WORKBOOK

Roberta Osser Baum

Editorial Committee

Dina Maiben

Ellen J. Rank

Book and Cover Design: Itzhack Shelomi

Project Editor: Terry S. Kaye

Illustration: Bob Depew

Copyright © 2009 Behrman House, Inc.

Springfield, New Jersey

www.behrmanhouse.com

ISBN: 978-0-87441-829-3

Manufactured in the United States of America

LESSON 1

Use after Lesson 1 in *Alef Bet Quest*

שֶׁמֶשׁ

Shin שׁ שׁ

Follow the arrows to write the letter.

 e e e e e e e e e e e e e

Trace the letter.

e e e e e e e e e e e e e

Write the letter enough times to fill the whole line.

e

Write the letter and vowel combinations.

e   e

Script Note

Throughout the book always write in Hebrew script. Try to write as many letters, words, or phrases as you can to fill the blank lines.

Follow the arrows to write the letter.

Trace the letter.

Write the letter.

Write the syllable.

Write the word.

Ḥanukkah Lights

Write the word שַׁמָּשׁ in script above the helper candle.

Write the numbers 1–8 above the other candles. Begin on the right.

Final Mem ם ם

Follow the arrows to write the letter.

ם ם ם ם ם ם ם ם ם ם ם ם ₂ם¹

Trace the letter.

ם ם ם ם ם ם ם ם ם ם ם

Write the letter.

ם

Write the word.

מֶם

Shaping Up

Write the letter שׁ inside each triangle.
Write the letter ם inside each circle.

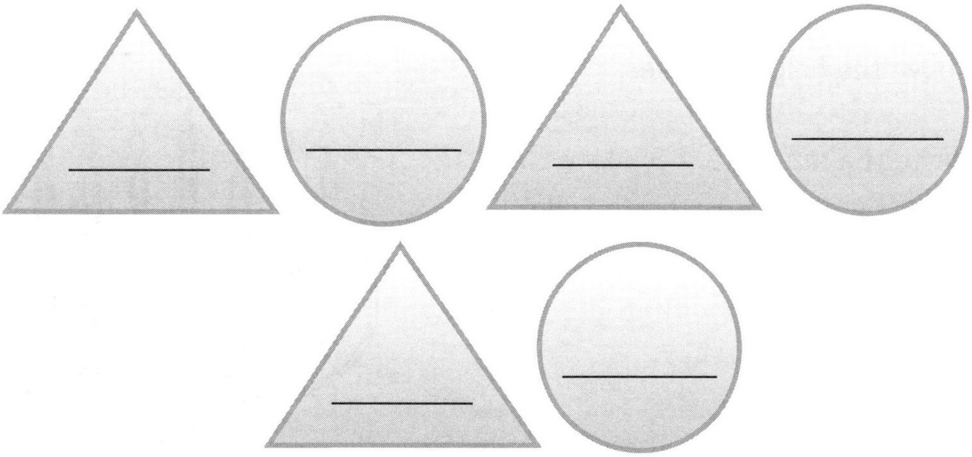

A Miracle

The four letters on the dreidel — שׁ ה ג נ — stand for the sentence:

A Great Miracle Happened There

The שׁ represents the Hebrew word for "there."

Which word means "there": שֶׁמֶשׁ or שָׁם? Write it here. _____

Where was "there"? Write your answer in English. _____

Change Over

Change each letter into script.

____ ם   ____ שׁ   ____ מ

Change מ into Final ם.

| _____ | _____ |
| Final Mem | Mem |

In Place

שׁ מ ם

Which letter can appear only at the end of a word? _____

Which letters can appear at the beginning of a word? _____ _____

LESSON 2

LETTERS YOU KNOW: אֶבָּא

Bet בַ ב

Follow the arrows to write the letter.

Trace the letter.

Write the letter.

Write the syllable.

Write the word.

Follow the arrows to write the letter.

אָ אָ אָ אָ אָ אָ אָ אָ אָ אָ אָ אָ

Trace the letter.

אָ אָ אָ אָ אָ אָ אָ אָ אָ אָ אָ אָ

Write the letter.

אָ

Write the syllable.

אָ

Write the word.

אָבָא

Write the phrase on each line.

בָּע אָבָא

בָּא אָבָא

עַם

Ayin ﬠ ﬠ

Follow the arrow to write the letter.

ﬠ ﬠ ﬠ ﬠ ﬠ ﬠ ﬠ ﬠ ﬠ ﬠ ﬠ ﬠ

Trace the letter.

ﬠ ﬠ ﬠ ﬠ ﬠ ﬠ ﬠ ﬠ ﬠ ﬠ ﬠ ﬠ

Write the letter.

ﬠ

Write the syllables.

ﬠֶ

ﬠ

Write the phrases.

ﬠַﬠֶ ﬡוֹﬡַ

ﬠַ ﬠֶﬠ

Write the two letters that make no sound. _____ _____

Silent Partner

Only one letter in each pair below makes a sound. Write it on the blank line.

ע ם ____ .4   ם א ____ .1

א שׁ ____ .5   ע ב ____ .2

א ב ____ .6   ע מ ____ .3

Connections

Connect the Hebrew letter to its name.

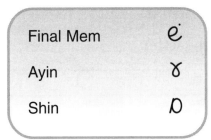

Alef	ב
Bet	N
Mem	אC

Final Mem	e·
Ayin	ע
Shin	ס

Connect the matching letters.

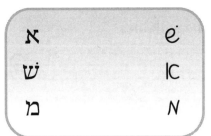

ם	ב
ע	ס
ב	ע

א	e·
שׁ	אC
מ	N

Use after Lesson 3 in *Alef Bet Quest*

LETTERS YOU KNOW: ℓ ℸ ◖ ◖ ℶ ℶ

אָדֹם

Dalet ℸ ד

Follow the arrows to write the letter.

Trace the letter.

Write the letter.

Write the syllables.

Follow the arrows to write the vowel.

Trace the vowel.

Write the syllables.

בוֹ

בֹ

Write the word.

כֹּאֹבֹ

What's Missing?

Write the missing letter in each script pattern.

___ N N ם מ מ .4		IC ___ IC א ד א .1	
ƺ ƺ ___ ד ד ד .5		ƴ ℓ ___ ע שׁ ע .2	
ם ___ ƴ ם מ ע .6		___ ƺ ƻ ב ד ב .3	

Lamed ל

Follow the arrows to write the letter.

Trace the letter.

Write the letter.

Write the word.

שָׁלוֹם

Transfers

Transfer each word and phrase from print to script on the lines below.

אָדָם   שָׁלוֹשׁ   עוֹלָם

_____   _____   _____

אָדָם לֹא שָׁם.   שָׁלוֹם אַבָּא.

_____   _____

Sounds Like

Use Hebrew letters you know and the vowel וֹ or ▆ to write words that sound like English.

show _____ low _____ bow _____

oh _____ dough _____ mow _____

Tic-Tac-Toe

Write the syllables below in script in the blank Tic-Tac-Toe grid.
Play Tic-Tac-Toe with a classmate. Write X or O in each square when you read the syllable correctly. Play again, this time using the syllables in print form in the grid on the right.

אָ	מוֹ	בוֹ
שָׁ	בֶּ	לֶ
לוֹם	דֹ	עֲ

Hebrew Names

Write each Hebrew letter above its name.

ע ל ב שׁ ד ס ם ד מ א

_____   _____   _____   _____
Mem   Alef   Lamed   Shin

_____   _____   _____   _____
Bet   Dalet   Ayin   Final Mem

LESSON

Use after Lesson 6 in *Alef Bet Quest*

LETTERS YOU KNOW: e ץ ם N ל צ ב כ lc

Yud ' י

Follow the arrows to write the letter.

Trace the letter.

Write the letter.

Write the words.

צְ   טְ

טוֹ   יָאֶר

אֶל   יָבוֹ

Follow the arrows to write the letter.

Trace the letter.

Write the letter.

ה

Write the syllables.

הֶ   הֹ   הִ   הַ

Write the words.

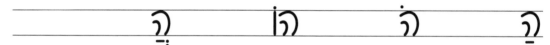

הַכּוֹכָם   הִיָּד

Handshakes

Read the word on each hand to your partner. Then ask your partner to
read the words to you. Handshakes all around!

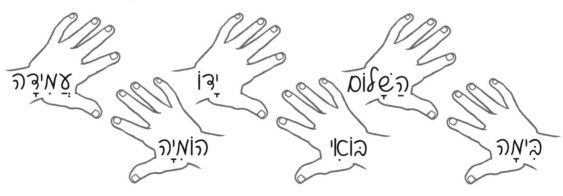

Gimmel ﬤ ﬕ

Follow the arrows to write the letter.

ﬤ ﬤ ﬤ ﬤ ﬤ ﬤ ﬤ ﬤ ﬤ ﬤ ﬤ ﬤ

Trace the letter.

ﬤ ﬤ ﬤ ﬤ ﬤ ﬤ ﬤ ﬤ ﬤ ﬤ ﬤ

Write the letter.

ﬤ

Write the words.

גָּמָל   בֶּגֶד

גּוֹזָל   עוּגָּמִים

גָּדָה   הוֹשִׁיעָה

Alef Bet Know-How

Write the first five letters of the alef bet.

ה   ד   ג   ב   א

____ ____ ____ ____ ____

Which of these letters makes no sound? ____

Word Cards

Write the correct word on the matching word card.

7. גּוֹאֲלִי	5. גָּדוֹל	3. הוֹשִׁיעָה	1. דֶּגֶל
	6. הַיּוֹם	4. אִמָּא	2. אֲדָמָה

_____
5

_____
1

_____
7

_____
3

_____
2

_____
4

_____
6

Weather Watch

Write the script form for each word in your weather dictionary.

rain	_____	גֶּשֶׁם
sun	_____	שֶׁמֶשׁ
snow	_____	שֶׁלֶג

Which Hebrew letter appears in all three words? _____

LESSON 5

Use after Lesson 9 in *Alef Bet Quest*

LETTERS YOU KNOW:

ﬠ ﬦ ﬥ ﬡ ﬨ ﬤ ﬣ ﬢ ﬠ ﬜ שׂ ﬨ ײַ ﬩ ﬡ

מַצָּה

Tzadi 3 צ

Follow the arrows to write the letter.

3 3 3 3 3 3 3 3 3 3 3 3

Trace the letter.

3 3 3 3 3 3 3 3 3 3 3 3

Write the letter.

3

Write the syllables.

צוֹ   צֶ

Write the words.

מוֹצִיא   מַצָּה

What Am I?

I am dough that did not have time to rise because the Israelites were in a
hurry to leave Egypt. I am _____ .

Final Tzadi ץ

Follow the arrows to write the letter.

Trace the letter.

Write the letter.

Write the words.

צֹום נ'ץ

צִיּץ ץֵץ

Finally!

Add Final Mem to each word.

____ שָׁלוֹ ____ קַיּוֹ ____ כֹּלַ

Add Final Tzadi to each word.

____ בֹּ ____ אַ ____ נ'

19

Resh ר ך

רֶגֶל

Follow the arrows to write the letter.

ר

Trace the letter.

ר

Write the letter.

ר

Write the words.

כַּרוֹב   גֶּרֶל

רֶכֶל   בֵּיצָה

Twinning

Find the matching pair of print and script letters on each line. Write the letters in the twin shapes. Example: ןc א

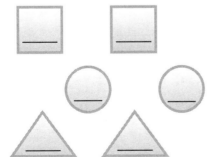

 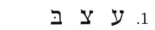
ם 3 e̊   ב צ ע .1

ׇ3 ר ל   ה א ד .2

ף ל א   ץ י שׁ .3

Follow the arrows to write the letter.

Trace the letter.

Write the letter.

Write the words on each line.

הַבִּיט   טָעִים

טוֹב   טֶבַע

Names and Numbers

Write each letter next to its name.

_____	Tzadi	ר .1
_____	Gimel	ה .2
_____	Resh	ג .3
_____	Tet	ט .4
_____	Hay	צ .5

Follow the arrows to write the letter.

ת ת ת ת ת ת ת ת ת ת ת ת

Trace the letter.

ת ת ת ת ת ת ת ת ת ת ת ת

Write the letter.

ת ת

Write the words.

טַלִּית תּוֹרָה

צִיצִית שַׁבָּת

Sound Alike

Connect the letters that sound alike.

N	IC
ח	ם
ת	צ
?	ל

Which letters make no sound? _____ _____

Pictionary Player

Write each word below in script.

Create a pictionary by drawing each word.

Draw	Holiday	Write
	מַצָּה	
	יָד	
	תּוֹרָה	
	שֶׁמֶשׁ	
	טַלִּית	
	גֶּשֶׁם	
	מִיץ	
	אַבָּא	

23

Use after Lesson 11 in *Alef Bet Quest*

LETTERS YOU KNOW:

א ב ב ג ה ד כ ל מ נ ס ע
ת ש ר ק צ פ

הַבְדָּלָה

Vet ב ב

Follow the arrows to write the letter.

Trace the letter.

Write the words.

מַבְדִּיל   הַבְדָּלָה

סוֹבְרָהָם   טוֹבָה

Dot to Dot

Change each Vet into Bet: ב ב ב ב ב

Write Vet. _____   Write Bet. _____

Follow the arrows to write the letter.

Trace the letter.

Write the syllables.

וֹ | וְ

וֹ | וַ

Write the words.

וָוֹ | מִצְוָה

וֹדְ | וו

סֻכְּתוֹ | תוֹצְוֹת

Hebrew-English Dictionary

Read the Hebrew words above. Then choose from the words to fill in the blank lines.

    commandment   _____

    fruit we use to celebrate Sukkot   _____

    boy's name   _____

    the name of this letter: ו   _____

Samech ס ס

Follow the arrows to write the letter.

ס ס ס ס ס ס ס ס ס ס ס ²ס₁

Trace the letter.

ס ס ס ס ס ס ס ס ס ס ס

Write the letter.

ס

Write the words.

סָבֶּיָך סַבְתָּיָך

מְסוֹרָה הֵסִיט

Family Reunion

Read the Hebrew word for each family member. Then write the words above their English meaning.

אַבָּא סַבְתָּא אִמָּא סַבָּא

_____   _____   _____   _____
    Dad   Grandma   Mom   Grandpa

Sin שׂ שֵׂ

Follow the arrows to write the letter.

שֵׂ שֵׂ שֵׂ שֵׂ שֵׂ שֵׂ שֵׂ שֵׂ שֵׂ שֵׂ שֵׂ שֵׂ

Trace the letter.

שֵׂ שֵׂ שֵׂ שֵׂ שֵׂ שֵׂ שֵׂ שֵׂ שֵׂ שֵׂ שֵׂ

Write the words.

יִשְׂרָאֵל   הֶשִׂיב

שִׂמְחָה   שָׂבָע

Letter Know-How

ס שׁ שֵׂ

Which two letters sound alike? ＿＿ ＿＿
Fill in the missing letter in each word.

לָ＿וֹשׂ   בְּ＿תַ　נ   יִ＿＿רָאֵל

Sounds Like

The letters in each pair below have the same sound. Write each pair above its matching sound.

צ ץ   ת ת   בו   מ ם   ט ת   א ע   ס שׂ

—	—	—	—	—	—	—
T	M	S	T	V	TS	NO SOUND

Word Wiz

Write the number of the print word next to the matching script.

_____	קָאוֹס	1. בֵּיצָה
_____	מִיׁץ	2. רֶגֶל
_____	בֵּיצָה	3. מִיץ
_____	רֶגֶל	4. אָדֹם

What Am I?

Use the words in Word Wiz above to fill in the answers to the following questions.

1. I am the color of a tomato.

   What am I? _____

2. I am a refreshing drink.

   What am I? _____

3. I am found on the seder plate.

   What am I? _____

4. I wear a sneaker.

   What am I? _____

Ring Toss

Below are the letters you have learned so far. Choose the correct letter to write inside each ring. High Score: 21 points.

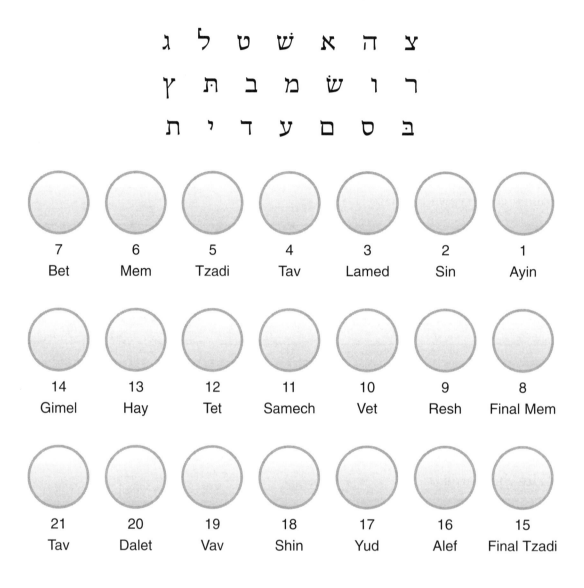

ג ל ט שׁ א ה צ

ץ תּ בּ מ שׂ ו ר

ת י ד ע ם ס בּ

7	6	5	4	3	2	1
Bet	Mem	Tzadi	Tav	Lamed	Sin	Ayin

14	13	12	11	10	9	8
Gimel	Hay	Tet	Samech	Vet	Resh	Final Mem

21	20	19	18	17	16	15
Tav	Dalet	Vav	Shin	Yud	Alef	Final Tzadi

Use after Lesson 13 in *Alef Bet Quest*

LETTERS YOU KNOW:

מ נ ל י ו ה ד ג ב ב א
ת ת ש ר ק צ ס ע

סֻכָּה

Kaf כֿ כ

Follow the arrows to write the letter.

Trace the letter.

Write the letter.

Write the words.

כְּלוֹ   סֻכָּה

כָּלָם   כּוֹסֵר

כָּתוּב   כֻּלוֹ

Koof קּ ק

Follow the arrows to write the letter.

Trace the letter.

Write the letter.

ק

Write the words.

קֶדֶק   קָבוּעַ

קָבוּעַ   מָקוֹם

A "Holy" Root

Words built on the root קדשׁ mean "holy," "sacred," or "set apart."
Write the two words above built on the root קדשׁ. Draw a picture of a
Kiddush cup under the name of the blessing that we say over wine.

_____   _____

Zayin ז ל

Follow the arrows to write the letter.

ל ל ל ל ל ל ל ל ל ל ל ל ל

Trace the letter.

ל ל ל ל ל ל ל ל ל ל ל ל

Write the letter.

ל

Write the words.

מְזוּזָה   לִין

יִזְכֹּר   מַזְמוֹר

This and That: This is script letter ג: _____   That is script letter ז: _____

Sensible Sentences

Write each sentence in script.

זְאֵבִי הַכֶּלֶב שֶׁל אָדָם וְגִילָה.

_____

אָדָם אוֹהֵב אֶת זְאֵבִי. גִילָה אוֹהֶבֶת אֶת זְאֵבִי.

_____

It's a Match

Connect the print letter to its matching script letter.

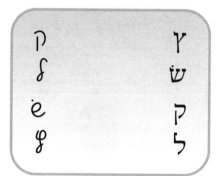

Which two letters sound the same? _____ _____

Shabbat!

Use the words below to fill in the blanks.

עֶרֶב הַבְדָּלָה קָדוֹשׁ הַמּוֹצִיא שַׁבָּת

Blessing over wine _____

Blessing over bread _____

Ceremony that concludes Shabbat _____

Two-word Hebrew phrase that means "Friday night"

_____ _____

Picture Perfect

Write the Hebrew word under its matching picture.

_____ _____ _____ _____ _____

See the Difference!

Write each Hebrew letter on the line above its name.

ס כ ל ו י צ ב ג ל ב ו י ס כ

_____ _____ _____ _____ _____ _____
Gimel   Zayin   Final Tzadi   Lamed   Vav   Yud

_____ _____ _____ _____ _____ _____
Bet   Kaf   Samech   Tet   Zayin   Dalet

Bingo for One

Write the number of each English word in the matching space on the card. The first example has been done for you. Now complete the card by writing each Hebrew word in script. BINGO!

1. sukkah	5. peace	9. Torah	13 hand
2. leg	6. mom	10. sun	14. grandma
3. rain	7. people	11. egg	15. tallit
4. matzah	8. Kiddush	12. mezuzah	16. red

			4
שָׁלוֹם	סַבְתָּא	רֶגֶל	מַצָּה
עַם	מְזוּזָה	אִמָּא	גֶּשֶׁם
בֵּיצָה	קִדּוּשׁ	שֶׁמֶשׁ	יָד
טַלִּית	סֻכָּה	אָדֹם	תּוֹרָה

LESSON 8

Use after Lesson 15 in *Alef Bet Quest*

LETTERS YOU KNOW:

א ב ב ג ד ה ו ה ל כ י ל ל נ מ
ת פ ש ע ק ר ש פ צ ש ס

מִשְׁפָּחָה

Pay פ פ

Follow the arrows to write the letter.

פ פ פ פ פ פ פ פ פ פ פ פ פ

Trace the letter.

פ פ פ פ פ פ פ פ פ פ פ פ פ

Write the letter.

פ

Write the words.

סֵפוּר כָּפָה

פִיל תָּפּל

פּוּרִים פֹּה

36

Follow the arrows to write the letter.

ח ח ח ח ח ח ח ח ח ח ח ח ח ח ח ח ח

Trace the letter.

ח ח ח ח ח ח ח ח ח ח ח ח

Write the letter.

ח

Write the words.

חַלָּה   מִשְׁפָּחָה

חָתוּל   חַיִּים

חָלָק   תַחַת

חַי   פֶּתַח

Short Takes

Write each sentence on the line below it.

כֶּלֶב בַּבַּיִת.   חָתוּל בַּבַּיִת.

מִשְׁפָּחָה לֹא בַּבַּיִת.

בְּרָכָה

Chaf כ ך

Follow the arrows to write the letter.

כ

Trace the letter.

Write the letter.

כ

Write the words.

בְּרָכָה   כּוֹכָבִים

כָּאכָה   מְחָאִים

כּוֹכָב   אֲכַתָב

Dot to Dot

Change each Chaf into Kaf: כ כ כ כ כ

Write each letter below.

Chaf _____   Kaf _____

Vet _____   Bet _____

Final Chaf כ ך

Follow the arrows to write the letter.

Trace the letter.

Write the letter and vowel.

כָ   כְּ

Write the words.

לְךָ   מֶלֶךָ

בָּרוּךְ   מֶלֶךְ

דֶּרֶךְ   כָּאוֹכָ

Sounds Like

Circle the three letters below that sound alike.

ת כ ה ך כ ח

My מִשְׁפָּחָה

Circle the people—and pets!—in your family. Then write all the words on the blank lines.

אַבָּא	סַבְתָּא	סַבָּא	אָחוֹת	אָח
dad	grandma	grandpa	sister	brother

_____ | _____ | _____ | _____ | _____

צִפּוֹר	חָתוּל	דָג	כֶּלֶב	אִמָּא
bird	cat	fish	dog	mom

_____ | _____ | _____ | _____ | _____

Sound Off

Connect the letters that sound alike.

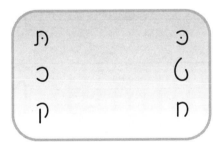

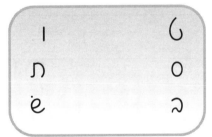

Picture Match

Write the name for each picture by choosing from the words below.

שֶׁמֶשׁ גֶּשֶׁם תּוֹרָה סֻכָּה חַלָּה מֶלֶךְ

_____ _____ _____ _____

_____ _____

Tic-Tac-Toe

Write the letters and vowels below in script in the blank Tic-Tac-Toe grid. Play Tic-Tac-Toe with a classmate. Write X or O in each square when you read the syllable correctly. Play again, this time using the syllables in print form in the grid on the right.

קוּ	פֶּ	זִ
לְ	סֶ	חֵ
גָ	כִּ	עַ

LESSON 9

Use after Lesson 20 in *Alef Bet Quest*

LETTERS YOU KNOW:

א בּ בּ גּ גּ ד ה ו ז ח ט י ךּ כ כ
ל מ ם ן ס ע פּ פ ף ץ צ ק ר שּׁ שּׂ ת

נֵר

בּ ן Nun

Follow the arrows to write the letter.

Trace the letter.

Write the letter.

Write the words.

נֵלֵכֵר   נֵס

נוֹרָי   נֵר

נוֹתֵנוּ   יָזְנוּ

Final Nun | ן

Follow the arrows to write the letter.

Trace the letter.

Write the letter.

Write the look-alike letters.

Write the words.

 זַיִן

יַיִן

שָׁוֹן

קָמֶן

Two Out of Three

Select the two letters in each set that belong to the same letter family and write them on the lines. Letter family examples: ס N   ב כ ך

____ ____ ב ח כ   ____ ____ ן ן ן

____ ____ ק ם ן   ____ ____ ם נ N

____ ____ ח ז ת   ____ ____ ב כ ב

43

Fay פ פ

Follow the arrows to write the letter.

פ פ פ פ פ פ פ פ פ פ פ פ

Trace the letter.

פ פ פ פ פ פ פ פ פ פ פ

Write the letter.

פ

Write the words.

סְפָרִים   שׁוֹפָר

כָּפֶן   יָפֶה

תְּפִלָּה   סֵפֶר

Dot to Dot

Change each Fay into Pay: פ פ פ פ פ

Write each letter below.

Fay _____   Pay _____

Chaf _____   Kaf _____

Vet _____   Bet _____

Final Fay ß ף

Follow the arrows to write the letter.

Trace the letter.

Write the letter.

Write the look-alike letters.

Write the words.

בוֹקֶ ß   אוֹßß

אוֹ·Oß   תֶכֶß

The End!

Write the final form of each letter.

ß ם כ ס ß ן

___ 3   ___ N   ___ ס   ___ J   ___ כ

45

Blessing Bee

Write the following blessing endings.
Draw a bee next to the line number each time you complete the phrase.

1. מְקַדֵּשׁ הַשַּׁבָּת

_____

2. הַמּוֹצִיא לֶחֶם מִן הָאָרֶץ

_____

3. בּוֹרֵא פְּרִי הַגָּפֶן

_____

4. שֶׁהֶחֱיָנוּ וְקִיְּמָנוּ וְהִגִּיעָנוּ

_____

5. לְהִתְעַטֵּף בַּצִּיצִת

_____

6. לִקְבּוֹעַ מְזוּזָה

_____

Pictionary Player

Write the names of the holidays below in script. Then draw a picture of an object that represents the holiday. Example: Draw a dreidel for חֲנֻכָּה.

Draw	Holiday	Write
	רֹאשׁ הַשָּׁנָה	
	יוֹם כִּפּוּר	
	סֻכּוֹת	
	שִׂמְחַת תּוֹרָה	
	חֲנֻכָּה	
	פּוּרִים	
	פֶּסַח	
	שָׁבוּעוֹת	

Which is your favorite holiday? _____

Special Sounds

Read then write each word below.

אָבוֹי   חֹשֶׁף   כְּכָל   עֵינָיו   תַּפּוּחַ   בְּמִצְוֹתַי

___   ___   ___   ___   ___   ___

Race Cars

Help the cars complete the race by writing the script form of each print letter below. Then say the name of each letter.